THE ART OF Being BROKEN

LIVE A HAPPY, HEALED AND COLORFUL LIFE: A COLLECTION OF TESTIMONIES

NOELLE HADDAD

Copyright © 2020 by Noelle Haddad Creative

All rights reserved. No part of this book may be reproduced or used in any manner without written permission of the copyright owner except for the use of quotations in a book review. For more information, email noellehcreative@gmail.com.

First paperback edition August 2021

Book design by Guglik Design

ISBN 978-1-7368895-0-3 (paperback)

ISBN 978-1-7368895-2-7 (hardcover)

ISBN 978-1-7368895-1-0 (Kindle)

www.noellehaddadcreative.com

Here we are—that part where you see who the book is dedicated to…

It's you! **You** *were the one I wrote this for.*

The one I prayed about while figuring out how in the world I would be able to write this book and said— "If this reaches just **one** *person. My mission will be accomplished." Thank you—you were an answer to my prayer.*

THE ART OF **Understanding
             & Promises**   1

THE ART OF **Asking**   33

THE ART OF **Testimony, Connection
             & Receiving Love**   61

THE ART OF **Pain**   75

THE ART OF **Forgiveness**   91

THE ART OF **Surrender, Vulnerability,
             & Trust**   107

THE ART OF **Prophecy, Words,
             & Dry Bones**   117

THE ART OF **Heroes
             & Inspiration**   131

A PRAYER THAT **Changes Everything**   140

THE ART OF **Writing It All Down**   145

UNDERSTANDING & PROMISES

I'm a dreamer,
a creative, and
a believer.
I would like to
add 'healing
agent and hope
ambassador'
to that list as
life goes on.

THE ART OF UNDERSTANDING & PROMISES

I do some of my best life work in these categories. I love people, a lot—and as I've healed through some of my life's pain I can now say that I love this life we have been given to live more than ever. I believe that each and every one of our collective stories matter. I started writing when I was teenager, and this last year I knew it was time to share some things that I've experienced with a larger audience outside of the pages of my journals and written prayers. I'm not a professional writer—just so passionate about putting out the message of hope—that if a broken little girl now woman, can make it through some of the mess that my life journey dealt me— yet still be a BIG dreamer, and want all the beauty that life has to offer, then I believe anyone can. I can't tell you how many times a message from someone else's story on more than one occasion was powerful enough to change my perspective, even oftentimes make me brave enough to carry on, though I, myself didn't think I could.

The power of our testimonies change the world.

I consider myself to be non-traditional in many ways, and fall into the all inclusive, and somewhat overwhelmingly complex 'creative' category. I only just accepted in my 30's that not fitting "in" with average norms of what culture says we're supposed to be when we grow up was a very beautiful thing. Understanding and still unpacking the unique gifts that God gave me has been an important milestone in my life. It took a lot of hurdles to arrive at true desire for the full acceptance of myself, as a person, and as an individual. I am still working on this in my journey. I remember the moment when it hit me right in the center of my chest—that God literally ***designed*** each and every one of us by hand, and with love and intention. All the intricate details and wonderfully different characteristics, quirks, talents, gifts,....from the color of our hair to the sound of our voice. Every freckle, every dimple, every laugh. How amazing to think—that we have a Creator—that we are all custom made by design, I could sit for months and just meditate on this unfathomable reality.

I thought I had to get a degree and stay in corporate America to utilize a college experience to be a successful person and have a happy or stable life. In the last decade of my life I've come to a much more peaceful place of understanding in who I was created to be. I'm still on this journey, and so I am forever a student. I wanted to put words to some of my experiences for anyone who may need it. It's with hope and total faith that I will inspire, or help anyone reading to *feel awakened to the hope and grace of God's love, his faithfulness, and his creative genius, not to leave out His restorational power.* He has a plan for your life no matter where you are or what you've been through. And he's a master *at making broken things very beautiful.*

You can come out of a completely dark and broken place and live a happy, healed, and extraordinarily beautiful life.

I would describe my childhood as somewhat of a trauma zone that was absent of light, healthy air and comfort. Because of my grim childhood experiences—I wanted to grow up fast and have fresh spaces to become and make new things of my life. I was always most comfortable while imagining or daydreaming what that looked like. I wanted to be surrounded by big skies and oceans. Bright sun, dreamy cityscapes, and lots of traffic.

Lots of views. Lots of celebration. Lots of color. Lots of art. And happy people from all over the world as my neighbors. I always felt like a global citizen, not a girl next door, or from any certain place. Maybe this is because I come from a long line of immigrants to this country, both on my Mother and Father's side. Having exposure of what it's like to be in a group of people that had to design their life from scratch, trying to embrace their culture, while given permission to dream, ambition and hard work to make it. My favorite magazine as a kid, was National Geographic. I would get lost in its pages of beautiful photographs. This may have been one of the first realizations of my deep love for photography, and wanting to see the world.

I wanted to get to a far away place. Far away from what home was. Even while struggling to understand my distorted reality— my hope burned for a better future.

I wanted adventure. I wanted freedom. I wanted to recreate my life, and my story.

That was it, most of my young life— this is what I prayed for.

THE ART OF UNDERSTANDING & PROMISES

One day I thought—Why was I always dreaming? Always in my imagination? Always hoping for something else.

Well....As a '30-something' in therapy working through childhood and adult trauma, growing up in a broken home, divorced parents, dysfunctional family, single parenthood, anxiety, repeating cycles, etc. I started to dig into this question. The digging became important. I knew the findings would give me direction ***if I was courageous enough to go back to places of pain, and try to face them, tend to ancient wounds, and find healing only God Himself could provide.***

Have you ever considered who you are, what you love, what makes you happy, what hurts most or gives you the greatest joy? What are your favorite things? What intimidates you, or brings you the greatest comfort? And is there a connection they have to your earliest life experiences? Have you taken the time to ask yourself some reflective questions about your life? Are you living in your purpose? Have you gotten off track, or lost your way? This is important work we all owe to ourselves. But it's important to understand that this is also important for others too. We don't always generously offer our hearts (or perspectives) in trying to know or understand our fellow brother or sisters life experiences. It can be a neighbor or even a co-worker. The people that surround us every day. They've all come with a story, of experiences. Ones that they had absolutely no control over. Economically or emotionally. Especially in the world we live in today—understanding how we are shaped from and during our foundational years of life—can make a significant impact on how our worldview is and how we treat others. This applies to relationships of every kind. No matter your vocation, background or tribe. It can offer insight to how we end up choosing and deciding on the important chapters of our life. This discovery and journey backwards was a part of learning how to truly love and care for myself, and ultimately for others in a different way. It opened up my heart to seeing myself through a clearer lens, and to feeling things I had wanted to numb for so long.

Sometimes we get so caught up in the expectations of the future, the ever present hectic schedules of life-we don't see the value in slowing down to learn our own history or our condition at its core, and to do the healing work of understanding who we really are. Who our personhood is. *You, as a person, an individual, MATTERS.* I can't think of a more appropriate time in history where caring enough about understanding ourselves and each other may be the greatest of tools we can responsibly use towards creating unity in our world.

Back to the days of my youth, I'm convinced I was praying for these things I called my dreams (and ultimately ended up manifesting some) because, I was so deeply broken. Maybe something very big and unknown would be the safest thing. The good part of life. The life I thought was available. Because the life of my home and familiarity was an unhappy world for many years since the beginning of my memories. Although I have wonderful memories as well, a lot of the wonderful was mixed with the broken. We don't get to choose the family we are born into, or the circumstances surrounding our childhood. But we do get a chance to create our own, and deal with what we've lived through in either a healthy or unhealthy way.

By daydreaming and always looking outside of myself, I was subconsciously fixing all that was wrong with the little girl inside that felt so much pain. But there was this one thing I knew. I knew I belonged to God. If I didn't know anything else. There was an awareness of Him. Since my earliest thoughts I'm able to remember this tender awareness as well.... I always I kept this with me, and would carry it for years to come. This was a key for my journey. Freely given to me, a gift of GRACE for my future. I must make mention of the underrated importance of the local church, and the impact that it had on my life. Yes, my Pastor's and Youth Pastor's prayers, even church family & friends that I know prayed for me…well—I believed I lived and overcame partly because of them. They were silent ambassadors that fed my spiritual journey. They were the seed planters for my future, and over the course of my life God was faithful to water them, and grow me. I had one family friend—who I'm still in touch with to this very day—she held prayer meetings at her house. I remember going there, not to pray (our parents did that) but to play with friends all night, while our parents prayed—some of the best times. I think about all those nights of prayer, and all those services I sat at, the youth nights, summer camps, and people just praying & loving all over my life. The lifelong impact that it had, even when I didn't recognize it, and was unaware of its lifelong power.

I held on to my awareness of God for dear life at times as a troubled adolescent. It was my safe place. He was my safe place. He was wonderful, sweet and magical to me. I would cling to Him. It was unshakable. It was poetic. And it was a truth that was buried and planted deep into the fabric of who I was. I didn't know why, or where it came from at the time. Back to growing up on a pew, walking down the block to church every Sunday, singing my heart out during worship services, running up to the altar and praying to a God I hoped heard me? Every message, every "church hug" every song and every prayer, it counted BIG. But back then-I didn't know the magnitude of this lifelong impact. I just knew His presence. Did you ever feel a sense of the mystery of God? Or the power of His love resting on you? Something outside of yourself, so grand, yet no words to put to the thoughts? A knowing that God was there? He was. It's Him and that is more than a feeling. It's His love. This is so important in my story. Just that simple, unexplainable love. God's presence—it never left my life. No matter how far off I drifted—and ran. That love was never too far out of my reach. It gently tiptoed behind me like a shadow, and covered me like cloud of unknown glory.

A little more of my history to help explain my foundation, I don't want to cry on the pages of this book but hope to connect to the broken parts of your story. We all have broken chapters. While we don't all share them with each other. My hope is to start the conversation of normalizing the sharing part and undoing the shame that someone might hold against themselves.

In the Bible it says

> *"And they have defeated him by the blood of the Lamb and by their testimony. And they did not love their lives so much that they were afraid to die."*
>
> Rev 12:11

THE ART OF UNDERSTANDING & PROMISES

That means that the word of our testimony is connected to how we overcome! So sharing my story, and you sharing yours—becomes a tool other people need for their freedom, healing or victory! That's powerful. That's good news. That's inspiring! Your story might be all someone needs to hope again, and find courage to keep going. I'll even go as far to say YOUR STORY could SAVE someone's LIFE.

I was born into a divorce. Synonymous for a life sentencing to dysfunction, right? We all know too well, and have heard the recited statistics. Unfortunately all too common and familiar to so many. Now you can google the research about single moms, trauma suffered by women, teenage pregnancy, divorce, ethnic disparities, the endless statistics. So from a stat standpoint, things weren't looking good for me. In fact the odds were stacked, and stacked high. This is why my story, even to myself is still so fascinating. I don't fit the status quo. Every bit of research and data, if true, has me currently in a completely different place than I am in living now. Another way to put it—my journey of collective experiences defied statistics.

Another reason I penned this book was to share that the statistics *didn't* determine my outcome. It is my hope to challenge you, in a moment with the thought that this is true for you too.

What if you were intentionally designed to defy every hurdle in your life?

What if ALL of your collective experiences, even all the painful ones are shaping an incredible and actual better version of you?

What if God's promise that He will take everything meant to break, or destroy you and will use it to recreate an even more beautiful story of your life, is actually TRUE?

What if waiting patiently and hoping courageously are huge keys to your future?

What if your pain and hopeless set of circumstances can propel you into total victory?

And what if your pain is meant to help set someone else free?

THE ART OF UNDERSTANDING & PROMISES

"Nothing can stop God's plan for your life." Isaiah 14:27

Understanding HIS plan Vs. Mine. That would become another key in my overcoming. Wow. This took a lot of learning the hard way to fully accept. God's plans, ways, thoughts, intentions, power, wisdom, and any other characteristic of who He is ...is just much greater. Greater than all things we can possibly come up with.

Who doesn't want a happy and successful life? It's what we love about the *American Dream*. Work hard enough and you can enjoy many prosperous and comfortable days. While there is nothing wrong with hard work and nice things, many who have faith in Jesus Christ have confused the plans that God has for us with the world's definition of prosperity. We then get discouraged when life is hard, and God's plans don't seem good. In these moments when I've been tempted to get discouraged about things that have happened over the course of my life, I've found I need to go back and take a good look at what God has revealed about his agenda for me in his word, the Bible.

THE ART OF BEING BROKEN

My mother and father were in process of ending their marriage by the time I came into the world. Their whirling love story started while my mother was a waitress at a popular Middle Eastern restaurant Pittsburgh, and my father (born in Lebanon) was visiting family in the United States. He migrated to Sydney, Australia from his homeland of Lebanon along with 4 of the 13 siblings -but he had one sister that lived (actually migrated) to Pittsburgh with her husband's family from Syria, and their children.

Mostly all of my family came from and still are over in the middle east to this day. I am first generation on my father's side. My mom was a beautiful Lebanese American girl, with a seemingly picture perfect childhood. My grandfather worked hard to provide for his family, and my mother was his princess. And goes the story she was treated as such, spoiled and had everything she ever wanted. I remember the talk of private schools, horses, sports cars.. I'm sure you can fill in the rest. Behind all of this, I'd come to find out later—things weren't as great as I thought. Picture perfect, but there were family issues—I only learned about far down the line.

THE ART OF UNDERSTANDING & PROMISES

My mom and dad....(from what I understand) it was love at first sight. They married with my grandfather's blessing—and she moved to Australia with him on their quest to start a family and enjoy their new beginning. When my mother realized she was pregnant with me she decided to come back to the US for my birth—so I could have American Citizenship, and also to be surrounded by her family and support system for when I would be born. He promised to follow her out after tying up ends with his job, and he never did. It was the beginning of the end. He never showed up in fact, my mother discovered he was having an affair .... he wouldn't be a part of my story until I was 14 years old. Under less than perfect circumstances.

My mother never recovered from this chapter of being broken, this was an open wound that directed many upcoming years. I remember her telling me that she still loved my father, and how much I was like him at a very young age. Whatever that may have meant. I certainly didn't know why she said these things—but they had significance as a kid on my memories. I just knew something about me being like him, looking like him, or just in general caused a storm of pain in her. I know it was hard for her to not be reminded of this pain, when being with me. Yes, that's how much it hurt.

She remarried when I was age 3—and life went on in a dysfunctional way. There were present struggles with mental health in our new family dynamic. My stepfather was battling bi-polarism, depression, and other serious life altering conditions-possibly some I may never know the full span of. I believe my mother became depressed, struggled severely with anxiety and unhealed trauma herself. Their marriage was abusive, emotionally, economically, and environmentally. Unfortunately mental health issues, don't just trouble you. They affect the atmosphere of the home, and change the way the children function, and communicate, even simply exist. A massive disruption to the beauty of family life. It has generational effects. Mental illness is as life changing as a cancer battle, or any other serious health condition that can destroy a family without proper support, and interventions. My brother and I were exposed to lasting and damaging effects of emotional abuse, abandonment, self parenting, leading to the disruption of our growth and wellness as developing children.

Growing up seeing this, and experiencing it first hand it has made me very passionate about people normalizing the mental health issues we face in our culture. The conversation of admitting you need help and being able to obtain that help, without anything being in the way of that. No stereotypes, no shame. Just freedom to receive whatever you need to live your best life whether you have a physical, emotional or mental need. Unfortunately in the 80's and 90's there was an even deeper stigma of shame than there is today with mental health. You didn't really talk about this with people that were close to you, there was no hashtag that highlighted awareness and resources for it. I will always be an advocate within my sphere of friends, colleagues, and family to help normalize treatment, acceptance, therapies, medications and most importantly conversations that make it safe to get the help that someone may need.

So because my formative years were built in an environment that took a lot of my innocence and happiness away due to things outside of a child's control—I had to carry things into the future that I never chose. Growing up in an unhealthy or abusive home whether emotionally, physically or any other way—leaves painful wounds that oftentimes need much tending to later on in life. You need a community of faith, support, direction, wisdom and love to surround your healing journey.

In sharing some of my own story, I hope to make you feel seen and heard. I hope that you feel empowered to trust and try again because another person said they did, and it actually worked. The truth is that you were made to come out of any broken place, and still have a beautiful life. And by made, I mean we were actually created to heal, and win!

That truth is found all throughout scripture.

If you don't have any faith left, or never had it at all you can borrow mine. When I ran to the end of myself trying to figure it all out—which was a very scary place—I ran to the arms of Christ. And as I continue to place my trust in Him, I begin to see a little clearer with every year of my life. I call it my 'Jesus filter'. And the 'Jesus Filter' shows me that these plans and love that God has for me (and you) are deeper and more satisfying than even my own ideas

THE ART OF UNDERSTANDING & PROMISES

about "a good life." Yeah, better plans than even my wildest and best dreams. Sounds crazy? It is crazy in a world that doesn't really run on this schedule. This isn't popular (yet) or mainstream. But I believe the day is coming very soon where the world will know and see what the love of God truly looks like. As humans we are running to the end of ourselves—as the whole world is experiencing pain or dysfunction in every corner and all at the same time.

And until that beautiful day arrives where everyone will come into this understanding—There's parts of the Bible that back this up.

The following verses have helped me gain a clearer grasp of how God plans to provide for my welfare, future, and hope. That is basically everything we need FOR LIFE! They help to change my perspective on my circumstances and helped me to grow in gratitude for the life of Jesus. The son of God came down, and wrapped himself in flesh …and took a walk in our shoes of humanity.

I choose to, by faith, believe in all of these promises. That doesn't necessarily mean that it will make sense in the natural world. It's a **CHOICE**. It's heart posture. Like when you take a new job—

that you think will be better for you, bring you more money and opportunity—you believe it. You take the chance—there's no guarantee—but by faith you just choose to go that direction with the hopes for a better life. Same thing—and I am here to say-I can tell you that He's never failed me yet. And like I mentioned before, if you don't have faith—Just borrow mine, for now. How many of the GREATEST success stories of all time require a risk to just believe in something that there is no guarantee for? … And we so willingly take that at face value. This choice of faith in Christ, the life that He lived and gave for me and for all—has been the best move I've ever made while being alive. Not one of His promises have ever fallen short—or been broken. Every single promise has or is actively true and becoming more real as life passes. In all of things I looked to, to pacify and help heal, or fix me nothing, not one thing has ever been as real, or infallible as the love I have found in Him, when I made the choice to believe.

If you can read these out loud, take a risk, a crazy step of faith—and believe them as the absolute truth. You only have something to gain, and nothing to lose.

God's Plan Regarding Your Wellbeing

God will provide every need.

"If God gives such attention to the appearance of wildflowers—most of which are never even seen—don't you think he'll attend to you, take pride in you, do his best for you? What I'm trying to do here is to get you to relax, to not be so preoccupied with getting, so you can respond to God's giving. People who don't know God and the way he works fuss over these things, but you know both God and how he works. Steep your life in God-reality, God-initiative, God-provisions. Don't worry about missing out. You'll find all your everyday human concerns will be met."

(Matthew 6:31–33)

God will send you the help of the Holy Spirit, so you are never alone.

"I'm telling you these things while I'm still living with you. The Friend, the Holy Spirit whom the Father will send at my request, will make everything plain to you. He will remind you of all the things I have told you. I'm leaving you well and whole. That's my parting gift to you. Peace. I don't leave you the way you're used to being left—feeling abandoned, bereft. So don't be upset. Don't be distraught."

(John 14:26)

God will make a way out of temptation.

"No test or temptation that comes your way is beyond the course of what others have had to face. All you need to remember is that God will never let you down; he'll never let you be pushed past your limit; he'll always be there to help you come through it."

(1 Corinthians 10:13)

God will provide you with His joy.

"I've told you these things for a purpose: that my joy might be your joy, and your joy wholly mature. This is my command: Love one another the way I loved you. This is the very best way to love. Put your life on the line for your friends."

(John 15:12)

God repays you for everything you've lost.

Jesus said, "Mark my words, no one who sacrifices house, brothers, sisters, mother, father, children, land—whatever—because of me and the Message will lose out. They'll get it all back, but multiplied many times in homes, brothers, sisters, mothers, children, and land—but also in troubles. And then the bonus of eternal life! This is once again the Great Reversal: Many who are first will end up last, and the last first."

(Mark 10:29–30)

God's Plan Regarding Your Future

God promises that one day you will be with him.

In my Father's house are many rooms. If it were not so, would I have told you that I go to prepare a place for you? And if I go and prepare a place for you, I will come again and will take you to myself, that where I am you may be also.

(John 14:2–3)

God promises that one day his work in you will be complete.

And I am sure of this, that he who began a good work in you will bring it to completion at the day of Jesus Christ.

(Philippians 1:6)

God promises that one day you will be like Jesus.

Beloved, we are God's children now, and what we will be has not yet appeared; but we know that when he appears we shall be like him, because we shall see him as he is.

(1 John 3:2)

God promises that one day you will see his face.

No longer will there be anything accursed, but the throne of God and of the Lamb will be in it, and his servants will worship him. They will see his face, and his name will be on their foreheads. And night will be no more. They will need no light of lamp or sun, for the Lord God will be their light, and they will reign forever and ever.

(Revelation 22:3–5)

God promises that one day he will wipe away every tear from your eyes.

He will wipe away every tear from their eyes, and death shall be no more, neither shall there be mourning, nor crying, nor pain anymore, for the former things have passed away.

(Revelation 21:4)

God's Plan For Hope

God gives you hope that you have a rich inheritance.

I do not cease to give thanks for you, remembering you in my prayers, that the God of our Lord Jesus Christ, the Father of glory, may give you the Spirit of wisdom and of revelation in the knowledge of him, having the eyes of your hearts enlightened, that you may know what is the hope to which he has called you, what are the riches of his glorious inheritance in the saints.

(Ephesians 1:16–18)

God gives you hope that the promise of the gospel is secured for you in heaven.

We always thank God, the Father of our Lord Jesus Christ, when we pray for you, since we heard of your faith in Christ Jesus and of the love that you have for all the saints, because of the hope laid up for you in heaven. Of this you have heard before in the word of the truth, the gospel.

(Colossians 1:3–5)

THE ART OF UNDERSTANDING & PROMISES

God gives you hope that death is not the end.

But we do not want you to be uninformed, brothers, about those who are asleep, that you may not grieve as others do who have no hope. For since we believe that Jesus died and rose again, even so, through Jesus, God will bring with him those who have fallen asleep.

(1 Thessalonians 4:13)

God gives you hope that you are not destined for anything but salvation

But since we belong to the day, let us be sober, having put on the breastplate of faith and love, and for a helmet the hope of salvation. For God has not destined us for wrath, but to obtain salvation through our Lord Jesus Christ, who died for us so that whether we are awake or asleep we might live with him.

(1 Thessalonians 5:8–10)

God gives you hope that you have been born again to a new life, one day to be revealed.

Blessed be the God and Father of our Lord Jesus Christ! According to his great mercy, he has caused us to be born again to a living hope through the resurrection of Jesus Christ from the dead, to an inheritance that is imperishable, undefiled, and unfading, kept in heaven for you.

(1 Peter 1:3–4)

God gives hope that you have seen God manifest in Jesus.

"He was foreknown before the foundation of the world but was made manifest in the last times for the sake of you who through him are believers in God, who raised him from the dead and gave him glory, so that your faith and hope are in God."

(1 Peter 1:21)

THE ART OF UNDERSTANDING & PROMISES

These are just a few of the scriptures that break down God's plans for us concerning our well being, His provision, and the future hope we have in Him!

Asking

What's your favorite quote?

I don't know that I have a favorite, because I have so many, but this one is at the top of the list. And the author is unknown.

> *"Questions are the root of everything great I have done in life. The most creative ideas ever experienced are often conceptualized by asking questions."*
>
> —Author unknown

There was a day that changed everything in my life around. Have you ever had a day like this? Maybe from your childhood, or even later on in life? A day that changed you at your core. These days are important to hold on to, they are powerful. Asking questions about days like this helped me to heal. When you are looking, seeking, or trying to find something, asking is key. And keep on asking even if you don't find what you're looking for at first. The 'keep on' part. I'd like to acknowledge that sometimes bravery is required to ask, and to keep on asking. You've got to dig your heels in the sand and be unmovable, with determination.

"Ask and keep on asking and it will be given to you; seek and keep on seeking and you will find; knock and keep on knocking and the door will be opened to you. 8 For everyone who keeps on asking receives, and he who keeps on seeking finds, and to him who keeps on knocking, it will be opened." (Matthew 7:7-8)

On a late afternoon, in my childhood home at age 14—I remember my mother's longtime family friend coming to pick me up in the back alley of where we lived. I was scrambling out to her car, wiping my messy tears, and trying to get myself together. She was a great lady—I knew she had known the depths of troubles going on behind closed doors in our family through my mother's eyes at least . She came to get me, and take me to stay with her after a disagreement I had, maybe the worst one I could remember with my stepfather. I vaguely remember what it was about but I know it was intense. My mother thought it was best for me to go to Australia to live with my biological father that I never met. Life was not good. I didn't know it at the time but, I was severely depressed, and incredibly desperate. I was trying to swallow emotional trauma that was unrelenting. I cried myself to sleep more nights than not. The dysfunction. The physical & emotional trauma was now about as normal as having breakfast in the morning. The alienation from all of my mother's family. The family I loved so much when I was around. My mother was not involved In her parenting most of the time, or when she was around-I never felt she was happy or present. My not well stepfather, a broken marriage, a long list of dark details-childhood dysfunction was officially kicking in as I hit adolescence. I was numb. Hoping God would provide a rescue. Being aware of how differently a young child processes things has softened my heart to troubled, mother or fatherless and disadvantage youth. I'm passionate about the work that is done at the community level for at risk teens. I know there is so much more work to be started. Awareness of the fatherless impact, and how this changes the structure of a culture is profound. It's women, and the children that are equally affected.

Just to take a moment to identify the facts, and realities that we face—as a nation. 19.7 Million children live in Fatherless homes in America, they say that almost all social ills facing America today are connected to this very issue. The number of children who grow up without a father in the home in the United States is concerning—I consider it a crisis. There exists a considerable research base that suggests that children raised in households lacking a father experience psychosocial problems with greater frequency than children with a father in the home. These problems have been found to extend into adolescence and adulthood and include an increased risk of substance use, depression, suicide, poor school performance, and contact with the criminal justice system. All of which I can attest to.

Lack of paternal involvement has also been associated with a higher likelihood of being bullied and experiencing abuse. To bring this into focus, there's ten adverse outcomes that may result from the absence of a father in a child's life: (1) Perceived abandonment, (2) attachment issues, (3) child abuse, (4) childhood obesity, (5) criminal justice involvement, (6) gang involvement, (7) mental health issues, (8) poor school performance, (9) poverty and homelessness; and (10) substance use. Children who grow up without their fathers may come to resent paternal-figures due to perceived abandonment. These feelings are real, and come from a lack of trust and result in a heightened sense of anger. As a child grows into adolescence and young adulthood, these problems may contribute to contact with the criminal justice system, substance abuse, as well as a variety of mental health problems. These consequences may result in interpersonal dilemmas including the inability to develop strong social bonds. For example, anger stemming from abandonment can make it difficult for juveniles to establish friendships and relationships. Hello to all the relationship problems we see

Attachment refers to the deep emotional bond that develops between a caregiver and a child. Children who come from a father-absent home are more likely to experience attachment-related problems than those from a two-parent household.

This may result in serious emotional issues throughout the lifespan. The inability to form a strong caregiver bond is associated with hypervigilance to anger and a misappropriation of hostility to neutralize their ability to regulate. Both of which result in conduct problems in the child. The consequence of creating difficulties in the development of friendships and healthy romantic relationships. The active involvement of a father with his children can promote empathy and self-control for a child throughout life. This is so profound!

Many publications have linked the absence of a father in the home to higher risk conditions for mothers and their children. Children that grow up in such households are much more likely to be the victim of physical (including sexual) abuse and neglect compared with those who grow up in a two-parent household. Children who grow up in a single parent home are twice as likely to be the subject of physical and/or emotional abuse. In addition, the absence of a father results in an increased psychological burden on the child, as he or she must make sense of why his or her father is not present. This burden extends beyond the child to caregivers such as the child's mother. Indeed, the needs of a child are hard to meet, even when a mother is very loving, committed, and caring. It's a task that carries incredible weight on the mother. God never designed a woman to operate in this role alone. I can testify to his reality as a single parent. When children are surrounded by multiple caring adults (e.g., mothers, extended family members, community members), they are more likely to thrive and feel supported. If the mother is the only caregiver of the child, mounting stress over the considerable responsibilities of parenthood may increase the risk of her harming her children or herself. There's so many angles, and avenues.

These are a lot of facts to carry without a lump forming in your throat or you heart sinking. I know every single mother reading these stats can relate to in some way, or another. Now while all these facts exist—I am proof of God's ability to resurrect the broken heart, all the way down to the biology of a child and make it brand new. Never can I ever underestimate the redemptive power of God's love.

I would call out to God, in the nighttime. Alone in my room. Just me and Him, and the night sky. I couldn't get enough of these moments. It was my favorite time. It was quiet. There was peace. No amount of silence with Him was enough. It was so good.

I could hear my heart, my thoughts, and I said my prayers with eager happiness, it was as if I always had great expectations of Him, Regardless of what life looked like. This was so natural.

> *I told God my dreams in those moments.*

I asked Him questions, I asked Him for everything I needed. I just kept asking. Like He was my father. I heard Him whisper to me. It was so soft, and so strong. It comforted me, it gave me a sense that He was so good, and that He was there. He was the best, and most faithful source of solace I had. This was God to me, it's who he was. It was sort of like my poetry, flowing and soothing to my soul. I felt like He was my best friend that listened, and was always close.

> *"In my distress I cried out to the Lord, and he heard me."*
>
> Psalm 120:1

Back to the moment my stepfather made me go outside that day, I remember I had no shoes on, I was left standing on the front porch. Which was close to the street we lived on. This felt so cold to me. It stood out so vividly, that I was shoeless, and my bare feet were on the ground. It was one of the most memorable parts of this moment. I think looking back as a child, it disrupted my ability to believe I was loved.

This is where the enemy can and did, in my case, insert a lie into my belief system. How many lies have we been bombarded with? How many untruths have you buried unknowingly along the way? Have you ever taken the time to simply ask yourself if you believed something that wasn't even true about yourself? I have learned the art of asking, and its power. Not that I've always gotten the answer I've wanted, or even on the first try. That's where God's word set me free. One day in reading that verse in Matthew—the "keep On asking' part jumped out at me like I never saw it before.

To finish the story—I walked around the side of the house, went down the cement steps that led to the basement door on the back side of our home. I went inside and I called out to my mother upstairs. She opened the door at the top of the steps looking down at me and said Kathy was coming to get me. I think in this moment there was a severing. That was the last time I would ever be at home. The last time I ever would do life with my mother. I would leave behind my baby brother-whom I adored. He was all of my sunshine, the purest love I ever felt, his little life was such a gift of warmth to me...These were little to my knowledge—my last minutes there. I had no idea that when my mom mentioned sending me to Australia, that it would later would be my fate. I thought it would go away, it was too extreme—she wouldn't, she couldn't right?

A few weeks later—I found myself listening to the Butterfly album after boarding a 24 hour flight, coasting above the clouds into the unknown. One layover in LAX. And then onward to Sydney. That numbness was kicking in again. I couldn't feel anything freely—just holding my breath. It was an urgent sense of adrenaline that I was trying to bury. I vaguely remember what I was saying—but there I was talking to God again... He was the only one I had important conversations with, after all. So I mumbled all my fears and asked Him to help me get through that flight. Somehow I knew He was listening on that plane. I asked Him so many questions, I didn't expect any actual answers. I just wanted to know why, and how, this was going to get better. There came a point in time where He started talking back—and answering. Everything. I now know He was always talking. It was just my ability to hear Him wasn't there, yet. He whispered gently to my heart that He was there with me—and He would never leave. Sometimes I believed this, and others I didn't. But at that moment I did. I told God I was giving Him my brokenness.. I didn't know what that meant, I just knew I wanted Him to have it.

I landed in Australia with a sense of innocent wonder. All of the racing thoughts I had of who my father was, or who he could be—would be placed to the test. After an awkward introduction and some time spent, it led to expectations being crushed. I ultimately didn't settle into Australian life after very long. I wanted to get back to my America, and due to cultural Arabic ways—my father wasn't letting me get back to the USA anytime soon, actually in his words not ever. I was incredibly homesick. I felt like life had tossed and turned me inside out. My mother wasn't on board to bring me home. She said I didn't have a home to come back to now. My grandparents, Aunt and Uncle, and other family members—tried their best to intervene and bring me back-—Until then I leaned into and enjoyed as much of the good moments of life I could. Between my adventurous cousins, touring around this new countryside and exotic climate, I was distracted enough to suppress my real feelings. I became quite good at this. It was always something I had to do.

In running around this new countryside—it was then I fell in love with the modern architecture of the city, here my always burning desire to be in that far away place was realized. That was the part I loved. It seemed like a gift wrapped in pain. I reveled in anything my eyes could see. I would buy 10 throw away cameras at a time. We still had to develop film for photos at this time. It was 1997. There were no smartphones, Facebook or Instagram. Just a local pharmacy drop off that would get your pictures developed in a few hours. My fascination with Photography was birthed. I became passionate about pictures. I felt so connected to a need to capture everything visually beautiful around me. It took me away, and I would do anything to get a good shot. I would feel so proud of good pictures I took. It was like I had the ability to make something beautiful. To this very day I feel the same. It took me many years of my adult life to buy a professional camera, and actually start somewhere with my passion. There is a quote attributed to author Ursula K. LeGuin, "The creative adult is the child that survived." I relate to this on so many levels. From an early age, I used my creativity or appreciation for things created as a way to soothe. It always felt glorious and invigorating to play with a brush, fashion, or to color, whether on canvas with paint or a face with makeup. So God used my giftings therapeutically at the time, and as a ministry form later in my life. When I think of any great song, the best paintings, the most iconic artists—I connect soul and passion to their work. Usually there's a powerful story behind soul. And pain behind passion. My experience in Australia was a molding season, and the dynamic of meeting your father for the first time as a 14 year old girl really is a book in and of itself. I've had to go back and revisit this experience. I still have things to learn and ask about its impact.

It's been so empowering to ask myself many questions about who I am, what I've been through, and how it's molded me. It's been equally as powerful to ask for the help I need to sort it all out. I ultimately made it back to the United States after I asked my Grandmother, Aunt and Uncle back home to help me return ….and the asking never ended… to this day—I know that at some point I became better at being my own advocate, and love to advocate for others. I love that I'm still learning how to do this all these years later.

God can provide what you need—through YOU, and your own voice!

Sometimes we're looking outside for something that is within.

The Holy Spirit is our GREATEST advocate, and He lives inside of us.

Reflective Life Questions

What can I celebrate right now?

_____

_____

_____

What do I need help with that I've never asked for help with before?

_____

_____

_____

What is something I often think about wanting to accomplish?

_____

_____

_____

What am I passionate about?

_____

_____

_____

What are my most important goals? How can I get help achieving them?

_____

_____

_____

THE ART OF ASKING

What is something I always wanted to learn more about myself?

_____

_____

_____

What is my greatest strength?

_____

_____

_____

What is something I've been putting off?

_____

_____

_____

How can I love myself better?

_____

_____

_____

Love others better?

_____

_____

_____

What small tweaks can I make to make my life feel less stressful and more nourishing?

_____

_____

_____

What am I most grateful for in my life?

_____

_____

_____

Other than time or money, what do I want more of in my life?

_____

_____

_____

What's a cause that's important to me? Why?

_____

_____

_____

What is something I've always wanted to do, that I've never done yet? Is something holding me back?

_____

_____

_____

What brings me the most joy? The most pain? The most comfort?

_____

_____

_____

What is my greatest personal challenge?

_____

_____

_____

Who inspires me? Who are my heroes? Why?

_____

_____

_____

What changes can I make to my life today that would give me more peace?

_____

_____

_____

How can I help or serve others?

_____

_____

_____

What wisdom can I give someone else about life experiences I've been through?

_____

_____

_____

When do I feel most loved?

_____

_____

_____

What is my greatest memory or memories?

_____

_____

_____

What brings me the most joy, peace and happiness?

_____

_____

_____

What is the most empowering experience I've had?

_____

_____

_____

Fill in or create some of your own questions for yourself, that you may have never asked or answered yet....

THE ART OF ASKING

TESTIMONY & CONNECTION
RECEIVING LOVE

THE ART OF TESTIMONY, CONNECTION & RECEIVING LOVE

As a kid, how do you land stuck in a foreign country? How do you or any of us get seemingly "stuck" in any of the things that have taken us down a road we never expected. The next year of my life made me want to write a book. It was the first time- I looked at my life as an unfolding story. I didn't know how to process this reality, but it was a knowing that existed strong inside of my heart. I thought it was a story that might help or encourage someone one day. Here I am 20 some odd years later finally getting to it. Reflecting on that time, I believe that was the beginning of the healing that I was seeking God for. He was giving me a perspective outside of myself, and though many more seasons of trials were to come- this was a beginning of a revelation that would last. One **that our stories aren't just for us**. What if I could help someone to have hope—or feel like they weren't alone? I can look to God's word and see this explained in scripture. We overcome by the word of our testimonies. That means that our shared stories, our witness of overcoming—give us power to get through for someone else. That speaks to the magnitude of healing that comes with relatability.

Back to this word in Revelation again....I want this to stick with you.

"And they overcame him by the blood of the Lamb, and by the word of their testimony; and they loved not their lives unto the death." (Revelation 12:11)

When we know that we are not alone, and that others share in our experiences, it gives us power, and makes us brave.

Strength is manifested in community.

Burdens become lighter immediately when we tell them. Ever listened to someone talk about their life and thought 'Oh, someone else has been through that, too? I thought it was just me!' Finding similarities with other people helps us live happy and healthy lives. Your life may feel ordinary to you, but it might seem extraordinary to someone else. Every story shared is a chance to make someone feel less alone.

"People have been sharing stories since the beginning of time, even before we had a spoken language," says Paul Zak, PhD, a neuroeconomist at Claremont Graduate University in California who studies the brain basis of human connection. Zak explains that listening to an excellent story—"one that captures us, moves us, transports us"—triggers a specific cascade of events in the brain and body. First, our heart rate increases as our attention is piqued. As we continue listening, the brain is prompted to secrete oxytocin, the neurochemical known for its ability to promote bonding (between lovers or a parent and child). That release activates a sort of chill-out response throughout the body, lowering blood pressure, easing gastrointestinal distress, and, according to a 2017 Frontiers in Immunology review, possibly exerting antibiotic-like effects that promote wound healing and suppress inflammation. It doesn't matter whether the story is happy or sad, fiction or nonfiction, on audio or in print, Zak says. "If it gets you interested and gives you a reason to care, it can help make you healthier."

I don't know about you but I think it's truly amazing how God created us with all of these intricately knitted together details about how our bodies become healthier because of connection, and sharing. And everything in science lines up with biblical context. That is pretty exciting, and certainly builds your faith in Him.

Nothing can be accomplished in isolation.

We were meant to do life collectively. We all possess something that someone else needs. We all have unique gifts, struggles, passions, stories and backgrounds that serve those around us. No man is an island. A growing body of research shows that the need to connect socially with others is as basic as our need for food, water and shelter, writes UCLA professor Matthew Lieberman in his first book, "Social: Why Our Brains Are Wired to Connect." "Being socially connected is our brain's lifelong passion," said Lieberman, a professor of psychology in the UCLA College of Letters and Science and a professor of psychiatry and biobehavioral science at UCLA's Semel Institute for Neuroscience and Human Behavior. These research studies continue today.

I vividly remember when I traveled, while flying specifically above the oceans- there was such a strong awareness of a really big picture of this life and my story. And not that my part (my life) was so small it didn't matter- but the contrary. That in fact my life, our lives -were so significant and that all things have been woven together by something so powerfully bigger than you and I. I always feel God's presence in substantial environments, nature, bodies of water, and even created structural things. Architecture, amazing wonders of the world and so on... His nature is so grande and unfathomable—***we can see traces of Him if we allow ourselves to be still, and look at all that is around us,*** even the greatest things man made himself. He's a big God, with a big plan. I've learned that the enemy tries to use isolation as one of his greatest strategies. When you are isolated, you tend to think very small. Thinking small leads to less opportunities, less connection, and less awareness of truth. Imagine if there were all of these open doors, beautiful people, and resources to bless and change your entire -but you never get to them just because you were isolated.

I know there was a time where I believed the lie, that surviving was the most important thing I had to do. What a sad truth. But yes I bit the bait. To this day I have to fight the battlefield in my mind and even my schedule. Being connected to healthy people, keeps you in check, and keeps you accountable. It also welcomes the love of God in your life. Community attracts the Holy Spirit. The Bible says the Holy Spirit is present whenever believers gather together *(Matthew 18:20)*. A great example of this was the early church of Acts, which made a habit of meeting together, eating together, and worshiping together.

As a result, "the Lord added to their number daily those who were being saved" (Acts 2:46–47).

Now speaking of sharing our testimonies—I have to get to a tricky part of my story. So all of the religious people—if you're reading—you might to cover your eyes or shut the book. I could offend you. But only if you're one of those people. Hah! (Yikes) Yes I'm quoting all these scriptures, and I'm a follower of Jesus telling you of Gods great power, but guess what? I ran from Him. Yes! I wanted nothing to do with Christianity, or "Christian folks." I thought they were the most judgmental, horrible people on the face of the planet. I grew up in the local church, literally

THE ART OF TESTIMONY, CONNECTION & RECEIVING LOVE

thought it was the best thing I had going on at a certain point in my youth—but I ended up dumping my Christianity around age 18. I didn't come back to it until about 7 years later. I went on a "religious" excursion of my own. I dabbled with trying to uncover and "learn" about every other religion or spirituality system there was. I researched, met with people that practiced other beliefs. I thought at one point I was decided on choosing Islam or new age practices. I was intrigued by the Kabbalah. The list goes on. I hit a wall. The wall was—I didn't find a love story. Yes, as much at that time that I hated to admit it—there was nothing like the love story, and the scandalous grace I had known of Jesus Christ in anything I was taught of in other religions. But yet… Christianity was a full blown hypocrisy to me, right? Wrong. It was people. Imperfect humans were the culprit, and we are all imperfect. It wasn't the Jesus part. It was the people part.

I took circumstances (connected to brokenness) and applied them to the whole system. So completely relatable—but I had a change of heart. It took me running away, and getting lost—to be found again.

To my surprise, shock, and disbelief: I couldn't find something or anything to compare to the unconditional love of Jesus and a God that would send His own son just so we could be in love and relationship with Him?

A God that loved the human beings He created from His own heart so much, that He never gave up, and relentlessly pursued us in a totally scandalous love story kind of way. And He won't stop loving you, or trying to find you. These very words I am writing are proof that He is looking for your love, and wants you to know about it. He found me when I wanted nothing to do with Him. His love chased me when I ran away. And now when I look at my life all I see are memorials of His goodness all around me.

> *Without any doubt, I've been overtaken by His love. He loves us, He is for us.*

When you think of the human experience overall, we desire one thing universally and regardless of tribe, nation, or origins- there's something that connects us: we desire acceptance, and love. All of life long we will have a God shaped hole in our very being that only His perfect love can fill. We will never quench our need for this love until we allow Him to fill it up, over and over again.

Receive His love, freely. It is for anyone to have. To believe in love again—required me to receive His love. Receiving sounds much easier than it is to do, if you are broken. But it's the ONE thing I had to do.

Can you imagine that there's a God whose love you cannot earn, and no matter what you have ever done—or thought—or will do— He just wants to love you, and give you everything you've ever needed to be whole, healed and free. Free to live in abundance, and peace. I couldn't imagine this. I didn't see this. I didn't accept this. He showed up and gave me this. The day I chose in faith to just receive it, out of desperation, I knew I had I surrendered to the love of God. I surrendered myself vulnerably like a child, and continually sit at His feet in wonder and awe of how perfectly He loves the imperfect me.

THE ART OF

Pain

'I know what it is to be in need, and I know what it is to have plenty. I have learned the secret of being content in any and every situation, whether well fed or hungry, whether living in plenty or in want.' (Philippians 4:8)

You know the hashtag #lifegoals? This verse is my #lifegoals.

I want to be wholeheartedly content in any and every situation.

The only way that this is remotely possible is through the Holy Spirit, in our flesh this is not easily done. Which is why trying to continue living a supernatural life has become my new norm,...and even beyond normal—really essential. You may ask how do you live **supernaturally**? Or that may sound so strange and unrelatable—I may even sound crazy to you. I get it. I do. The worst thing ever is an unrelatable, Christian right? At least that's what I used to say...but how to live like this is another choice. A choice to surrender the things of this life and walk by faith. I have not by any means mastered this, or am perfect in dealing with pain or trials. I am human, and I do not for one moment want to deny my human experience. We shouldn't have to, after all God gave us this life to experience in its fullness. But part of living a full life is experiencing the spirit that is who you will be, forever—even when this body passes away.

What I will tell you is that I am grateful, grateful for having a realization that no matter what my body, mind or heart is physically going through—I can choose to walk in faith. I can choose to walk in healing.

I can choose joy.

I can choose peace. I have this option!? I'm afraid this way of life isn't that popular on self-help blogs. It doesn't pop up on google. And again, It's not mainstream. Not yet… but it is the most powerful key that God has ever allowed me to experience. Choosing by faith, to believe by the Spirit that no matter what is happening in the flesh—I can overcome it. Actually to push a little farther— it's already DONE!

Through Jesus Christ.

This is what salvation is. It's a gift. A free gift that was given. Who doesn't want a free gift? Of unconditional love? Christ gave His life freely for us, so we could be reconciled back to God our creator, the very lover of our soul. Why aren't we screaming this louder from the rooftops to every corner of the planet?! A holy God made us just for love and relationship with Him. The wildest, freely given love with no conditions on how wide and deep His love is for us, is in fact totally scandalous.

God didn't want us to be robots that forcefully walked around and worshipped Him like slaves. He gave us all a free will, to rule and reign over this planet because He wanted relationship. We messed up the original plan with the incredible amount of power He gave us to do as we wanted. As you can clearly see the state of the world today. We didn't do so well with all that freedom and luxury.

Human beings have done some spectacular things—but in the process—We've destroyed one another, we've warred since the beginning of time and now we're seeing we even ruined our planet. Today we are in a global crisis in almost every category. However, God loved us so much He saw us, saw our condition and said—I have to make another way for them to come back to me and have that relationship I wanted with them. And as far as I can tell throughout all of my digging up other religions—(I've explored so many)

> *Christianity is the ONLY love story in history between a God and a people that is based on the pursuit of love.*

Whattt!?? Spoiler alert: This is the greatest love story you'll ever hear. It's better than a fairytale. It's real.

Now does that mean that Christians are these perfect people and there's not a lot of bad, downright horrible folks that claim Christianity? No. I will tell you FIRST-hand. There are people that call themselves Christians. And they do terrible things. You can call yourself whatever you like, or identify with anything you choose—Sadly the world sees that, and it's been highlighting Christians as being some of the most judgmental and harmful people out there.

But along with good, we know evil exists.

We have an enemy and he would like for you to never know the truth about Jesus, and the greatest, purest love you could ever experience. He doesn't want you to know that if you're at your lowest, there is grace and way out. He wants us to think life is rigged, even impossible. He wants you to feel hopeless and ashamed of everything wrong you've ever done. He wants you to get stuck in your thoughts, trapped in depression and low self-esteem. If the enemy can convince you that you're worthless, or just keep you simply distracted, with the wrong friends, or influences he can rob you of your destiny. If you don't know who the enemy is—this is what he sounds like. So if you've ever felt any of those, or as if you can't go on, you're not good enough, or your pain is too deep and heart is too broken for fixing, then you've been attacked by his lies.

I want you to ask yourself—if you ever wanted to escape what they call 'the voices in your head' or life in general? Have you wanted to throw in the towel on your dreams? If you have— then welcome to the human experience—We have ALL been there, and that makes you nothing shy of perfectly normal! You are not alone. Not even a chance. I'm so confident in this, and I encourage you to reach out to a local church, or maybe it's a podcast you've felt helped you, a show on tv with a prayer line, a great friend, counseling service, or just a crisis number… and ask for support. I'm speaking to people who are in the thick of things. Maybe you're going through a divorce, death, career loss, medical diagnosis, broken relationships, financial troubles, struggling with addiction, depression, thoughts of suicide, abandonment, rejection, betrayal…

These parts of life are real. They happen to the best of us. No one is exempt.

There is a quote I absolutely had to mention by C.S. Lewis. He wrote a famous line in one of his books called ***The Problem Of Pain, "Pain insists upon being attended to. God whispers to us in our pleasures, speaks in our conscience, but shouts in our pain: it is His megaphone to rouse a deaf world."***

For me pain was the tool that God used to turn my life around. You know the saying 'I'm at the end of my rope'… well when I got to the end of mine—is where I found God. This is a common theme in humanity. When we are desperate, or have great need—our hearts are softened to help. So if the right or wrong 'help' presents itself—then we usually are inclined to it more than ever. Sometimes pain can lead someone more dangerously off track—as well.

I know that I used drugs, sex, relationships and alcohol to numb myself for a very long time. The pain I had suppressed instead of dealing with… led me to substance addiction. I was a regular cocaine user, a functional at times alcoholic, professional partier and serial bad relationship chooser. If it wasn't for God—I never wouldn't have made it off the floor of a bathroom in a strip club. I was so intoxicated that I was passed out—and barely breathing from the amount of alcohol that was flooding my bloodstream. I had to be taken out by a stretcher on an ambulance in front of all of my friends—and taken to the hospital to have my stomach pumped. That's not the only time something like that happened either. This lifestyle went on for years, I had to suffer so much heartbreak, from becoming a single mother, watching my health both physically and mentally deteriorate, for me to even begin to wake up to the reality that I needed serious help.

THE ART OF BEING BROKEN

I am in no way writing as someone who has accomplished the art of dealing with painful things perfectly, but I am writing to express that God can turn it around for you. I simply want to state that ***there is a beauty in the very essence of pain, there is a gift in it when it is encountered with patience and endurance—and there is a power in the overcoming.*** It seems paradoxical, but like most Christian truths, there exists a greater sense beyond human understanding. Some things are truly enigmas. Pain is at many times perceived as weak, evil, unnatural, something that should and must be avoided (and I am in no way advocating not to avoid it—i.e. to self-inflict or to inflict pain upon others). But there must be more than this, of how we explain or see pain to be. Some pain(s) remain for moments, others for years. What matters most is how we experience this pain and its journey of discovering ourselves through it. How do I see myself when encountering this pain and how do I react? Now it is easy to say 'analyze yourself' when going through a traumatic period, and one of the last things that may come to mind is to tell yourself to stop, reflect and question. But in order to free oneself from the lasting effects of pain and its imprint, there has to be a different reaction, a different way of understanding and experiencing it. We all go through it, we're guaranteed it. So let's run up to it and not cower back—let's fight it for its reward.

The ultimate example of how pain should be received, of course, is Christ. Not only through the view of the crucifixion (but this of course was and is beyond human comprehension of sacrifice)—but also throughout His ministry where He regularly encountered different forms of pain. Whether He was judged and questioned by the Jews (who first-hand should have known who He was, when your friends & family betray you), or when He wept over Israel for their unbelief, or when He was doubted and abandoned by His disciples—there was plenty of space for pain to be implanted and thrive in Christ's life. But He didn't allow that type of pain, that is psychological distress or anxiety or worry to harm Him because He knew who He was and is and was not shaken by temptations. So the way I respond to pain is linked with my identity—I know as a human there will be suffering and sadness and grief, and I know as a human I have a right to have emotions and experience different feelings, but how, as a human, should I channel these emotions and feelings? ***We are not merely human, but we are divine-imprinted humans, formed and made in the glorious image and likeness of the perfect God;*** the same One who showed humanity how to be human in Himself. If you want to survive being human well, you have to imitate Christ. Simply put, hard to imagine. He did it, perfectly.

This of course, sounds really idealistic and can be seen as illusionary or ridiculous. Some may say, Christ was only able to overcome pain because He is God and God, by nature, is impassable. Yes, but Christ being fully human, also took a soul and completely human body, —everything that is human He took to Himself and sanctified it. In this sanctification, He also sanctified pain. He turned the face of pain into a means of overcoming the evil of the world and sin; He transformed it so that if one undergoes pain righteously (that is patiently and offering it up to God), it will be accounted as a blessing. He promises to turn what was meant to hurt, and make it work for your good.

THE ART OF PAIN

"But even if you should suffer for righteousness' sake, you are blessed" (1 Peter 3:13)

It makes God sound like a sadist? I must experience pain so that I may receive a blessing. Not in that way. I naturally experience pain because of the brokenness of this world (pain whether caused by ourselves, others, natural events such as death, so on), but because I trust in the living God who is able to make all pain and evil into goodness, righteousness, holiness, this pain will become a transformative power—in becoming the power of pain.

A great example of this is my own life—is being a single mother. My greatest fear perhaps? Actualized. My greatest pains have been birthed out of moments of my struggles in this season, yet the most powerful healing in my heart & soul. The greatest of love, the best of memories. The most gruesome strength building exercises, and more tears than an ocean—yet their life has given me abundant life, and joy unspeakable. Their love changed my view of the world. While the circumstances have not been ideal and often terrifying, even caused me to feel shattered and hopeless— the blessing is greater. The blessing that was wrapped in pain, has been my best gift. God knew what He was doing even when I didn't. He took my poor choices made out of low self-esteem, and a broken past—and turned it around for my good. This is a promise He makes—and has never failed me yet. This is like a super dose charged shot of confidence for my faith in Him. He proves Himself faithful, over and over again.

Reflective Thoughts:

What is a painful experience or current circumstance that you can say actually made you better?

_____

_____

What did you learn?

_____

_____

_____

What wisdom came of it, or even the ability to help someone else because if it?

_____

_____

_____

Flip your pain into your POWER!

THE ART OF

Forgiveness

THE ART OF FORGIVENESS

Proverbs 17:9—Love prospers when a fault is forgiven…

I'm sitting in a local coffee shop as I begin to unpack and try to think about the most important things I've learned… and still am learning about the subject of forgiveness.

I think knowing what forgiveness is and isn't, equips us to do it much better.

I used to struggle with the word forgiveness. I thought that it meant I needed to not 'feel' a certain way if I truly forgave someone or even myself. I thought I wouldn't think about things that had happened, if I really let it go. So therefore—I thought I was incapable of true **forgiveness**. I was basing it off of a feeling. As I grew, and learned how to be gentle with myself through the process of healing; I came to understand that real forgiveness is a process. I walked through a phase of learning what this would like after becoming a single mother. One day in 2014, I was in a new category, I had 2 children, and was living on my own after separating with their father. I think single motherhood needs its own book—but to stay on track—I didn't want to accept that it was my reality, that I had to raise my children in a broken home, or alone. I didn't want to face that I had to swallow the crushed dreams and goals I had of my own family model, and the coparenting department, or what perfect picture I thought I'd be able to give them was now just a dead dream. I wanted to do everything in my power to provide them with all the things I never had. Starting with a really healthy home. And yet here I was. The black sheep in my circle, the only single unmarried in my sphere of support. I felt unrelatable, and I felt shame. I felt it within my family, my friends, and in my heart towards myself.

You might not believe it, but the number of households run by single moms in the US now make up 25% of the total. Single dads come in at 6%. Add the two together and that accounts for about a third of all American households. Sometimes zooming out and looking at the big picture can really help adjust your perspective. It can ease the pain and the challenges of being a single parent a little bit.

Although we (us single parents) aren't acknowledged very much as a thriving group of people—we cannot forget that the difficulties single parents face today are compounded by certain misconceptions and prejudices going the rounds. But there are so many happy memories and tender moments you will never forget. The closeness and bond I have with my children is incredible! I've made some kind of lemonade out of these lemons, and with all the challenges I see God's grace wrapped around me everywhere. Being a single mom is the hardest, most empowering thing I've ever done.

> *"Dare to live by letting go."*
> Tom Althouse

Back to the forgiving part... After you are wronged and the initial wave of emotion has passed, you're presented with a new challenge: Do you forgive the person? By forgiving, you let go of your grievances and judgments and allow yourself to heal. While this may sound good in theory, in practice forgiveness can sometimes feel impossible. There's no magical moment where all of a sudden it appears, it's actually a choice. A choice to keep choosing. A choice to silence voices in the battlefield of your mind and choosing to be free, from an offense or disappointment. Being free is a choice. Being free comes from the inside. Being free is the ability to choose that your healing and your overcoming is much more important, and valuable than holding on to pain.

Studies have found that the act of forgiveness can literally bring rewards for your health, lowering the risk of heart attack; improving cholesterol levels and sleep; and reducing pain, blood pressure, and levels of anxiety, depression and stress. I wanted to give my children, friends, and family the best version of myself—so I knew I needed some help with this. That's where the 'Art of Asking' connects to the other parts of my story.

The key word is in the phrase 'act' of forgiveness, did you see that? Act. Which means it's a verb. An action. Forgiveness frees us to live in the present... Our anger, regret, hatred, disappointment or resentment towards someone or something means that we are giving up our power to that person or situation. We need our power, we need our health, we need our wellness. God calls us to live abundantly and prosper in our health. Jesus suffered and died for us although we didn't deserve it so that we could have eternal life. He forgave us of our sins and remembers them no more according to Isaiah 43:25. As a result, we need to forgive others no matter what the situation may be, just look to the cross and remember what Jesus did for you. I had a moment with God where He showed me that forgiveness would be a lifestyle. It would become a way of thinking. The more you practice and are intentional about anything, the more you can do it with ease.

Forgiveness is at the core of emotional well-being. It is fair to say that holding on to unforgiveness can make people emotionally sick. The bitterness is a disease of the spirit, and it is inevitable that the unforgiving person eventually will experience physical illness as well. Anger causes surges of adrenaline and secretes other powerful chemicals that attack the body. The stress we carry when we refuse to give or receive forgiveness affects our hearts, minds, and bodies. I experienced this. I was walking around with wounds, bleeding on other wounds. I didn't know what this was until I became so desperate for help and I cried out to God for help. To make matters worse, both rage and depression contribute to obsessive behaviors such as overeating, workaholism, overspending, and even addictions to pornography and mood-altering drugs. We cannot rid ourselves of emotional pain and its side effects unless we are willing to forgive.

Unresolved anger keeps us from moving forward because it locks us in a time machine, frozen on the exact moment when a particular offense occurred. Fear of further injury makes us unwilling to move to new levels of relationship, not only with those who have hurt us but with anyone who represents a similar threat. Then I realized, when Jesus said we had to forgive 70 times 7… He was asking us to do something that is humanly impossible. In and of ourselves we don't have enough forgiveness to go around. But God does. So when our limited resources run out and we are unable to forgive, we can ask him to forgive others through us. In so doing, we take one more step of obedience and allow ourselves to **become a conduit of God's grace.** I absolutely love when God asks something of me that I can't accomplish on my own! That means I have to give it all up, and wait on Him.

That is the best place to be, expecting Him, and waiting for His manifestation power.

2 Corinthians 12:9—Each time he said, "My grace is all you need. My power works best in weakness. So now I am glad to boast about my weaknesses, so that the power of Christ can work through me."

Forgiveness is not letting the offender off the hook. We can and should still hold others accountable for their actions or lack of actions.

Forgiveness is returning to God the right to take care of justice.

By refusing to transfer the right to exact punishment or revenge, we are telling God we don't trust him to take care of matters.

Forgiveness is not letting the offense recur again and again. We don't have to tolerate, nor should we keep ourselves open to, lack of respect or any form of abuse.

Forgiveness does not mean we have to revert to being the victim. Forgiving is not saying, "What you did was okay, so go ahead and walk all over me." Nor is it playing the martyr, enjoying the performance of forgiving people because it perpetuates our victim role.

Forgiveness is not the same as reconciling. We can forgive someone even if we never can get along with him again. Forgiveness is a process, not an event. It might take some time to work through our emotional problems before we can truly forgive. As soon as we can, we should decide to forgive, but it probably is not going to happen right after a tragic divorce. That's okay. We have to forgive every time. If we find ourselves constantly forgiving, though, we might need to take a look at the dance we are doing with the other person that sets us up to be continually hurt, attacked, or abused. That's not always easy, but I aspire to get better at this task over the course of life. Forgetting does not mean denying reality or ignoring repeated offenses. Some people never will change. We need to change the way we respond to them and quit expecting them to be different.

Forgiveness is not based on other's actions, but on our attitude.

People will continue to hurt us through life. We either can look outward at them or stay stuck and angry, or we can begin to keep our minds on our loving relationship with God, knowing and trusting in what is good.

And the kicker—If they don't repent, we still have to forgive. Even if they never ask, we need to forgive. We should memorize and repeat over and over: Forgiveness is about our attitude, not their action. We don't always have to tell them we have forgiven them. Self-righteously announcing our gracious forgiveness to someone who has not asked to be forgiven may be a manipulation to make them feel guilty. It also is a form of pride. Withholding forgiveness is a refusal to let go of perceived power. We can feel powerful when the offender is in need of forgiveness and only we can give it. We may fear going back to being powerless if we forgive. For example Post-divorce problems related to money, the kids, and schedules might result in the need to forgive again and to seek forgiveness ourselves. We might forgive too quickly to avoid pain or to manipulate the situation. Forgiveness releases pain and frees us from focusing on the other person. Too often when we're in the midst of the turmoil, and we desperately look for a quick fix to make it all go away. Some women want to "hurry up" and forgive so the pain will end, or so they can get along with the other person. We have to be careful not to simply cover our wounds and retard the healing process. I did this for so long, again thinking I hadn't forgiven. But I did—too thoughtlessly. We might be pressured into false forgiveness before we are ready. When we feel obligated or we forgive just so others will still like us, accept us, or not think badly of us, it's not true forgiveness—it's a performance to avoid rejection. Give yourself permission to do it right. Maybe all you can offer today is, "I want to forgive you, but right now I'm struggling emotionally. I promise I will work on it."

Forgiveness does not mean forgetting. It's normal for memories to be triggered in the future. When thoughts of past hurts occur, it's what we do with them that counts. When we find ourselves focusing on a past offense, we can learn to say, "Thank you, God, for this reminder of how important forgiveness is." Forgiveness starts with that mental decision. The emotional part of forgiveness is finally being able to let go of the resentment. A sweet surrender. Emotional healing may or may not follow quickly after we forgive. But you can be sure that God will not leave you without His grace in the process. Through God's word we can find much understanding of what forgiveness means to Him.

Romans 5:8—But God demonstrates his own love for us in this: While we were still sinners, Christ died for us.

The above verse really helps me. We're all imperfect, we've all hurt others and we've all been hurt. Christ was the living example of forgiveness. We never deserved this love, we didn't earn it. It was a gift. The greatest gift given to humanity.

Reflective Self Question:

Is there anyone, (including myself) or any area of my life that I need to work on applying true forgiveness to?

_____

_____

_____

_____

Is a past hurt, or offense holding me back from true healing, and freedom to move forward?

_____

_____

_____

_____

THE ART OF

SURRENDER VULNERABILITY & TRUST

THE ART OF SURRENDER, VULNERABILITY, & TRUST

By definition surrender means to cede, cough up, deliver, give up, hand over, lay down, relinquish, render, turn in, turn over, yield

> *1a: to yield to the power, control, or possession of another upon compulsion or demand surrendered the fort*
> *b: to give up completely or agree to forgo especially in favor of another*
> *2a: to give (oneself) up into the power of another especially as a prisoner*
> *b: to give (oneself) over to something (such as an influence)*

Something really valuable I stumbled on one day—when you try to control something, or find yourself being more comfortable controlling than receiving, the root of that need or managing style is fear. Yes a control freak— is secretly or maybe blatantly—operating in fear. Control creates an illusion that you can manage the outcome. And for all of my fellow type A personalities out there—in all fairness, yes you can change how well or how excellent you do the things you do. Nothing wrong with great time management, operating in excellence, healthy ambition, discipline, hitting goals and the list goes on. But when we are holding onto hurt, or bad experiences, silently managing, suppressing pain, or creating impenetrable walls, to control the possibility of being hurt, seen or portrayed as weak… we've crossed a dangerous line and walked into some fear.

All around our virtual platforms of media—you are bombarded with the filters, photoshops, and edits. And while I love a good filter myself—for the aesthetic and sheer fun, sometimes I see even that is a form of me controlling how I'm viewed. We want perfection. We want people to see us as perfect. We are living in a culture where natural aspects of life, pain, or even aging are always encouraged to be camouflaged. I remember one day when I was a Professional MAC artist, I wanted to create a natural makeup application for this young lady, where we would let her natural skin, come through. She wanted nothing of 'Her Face' to show. She wanted full coverage and not a bit of her natural skin showing. It made me feel sad, that she didn't see her own beauty. Eventually I started to use the makeup chair as a place I give confidence and love away, in addition to a beautiful makeup application. I felt a tugging on my heart to make sure all of my clients felt a little more beautiful on the inside, along with the outside transformation they came for. This is why I named my makeup business Image and Soul. It's an inner and outer concept. Not one without the other, a "both" concept. Doing makeup for 15 plus years, I was so honored to be a part of so many women's stories that they shared with me while in my chair. This type of work, you get such an inside view of the common things we all struggle with, as human beings. You see the broad consistencies of how deeply we suffer with insecurity… and surrendering.

> *Being vulnerable in all of our imperfections to the one that loves us unconditionally, is the sweetest of surrenders.*

When we become a Christian, we've confessed our need and desperation for a Savior. We're letting go and letting God take control of our lives. This act is giving your life, and broken pieces, fragments, and imperfections to God. From that point forward, we have one foot on earth and the other one in heaven. We're essentially living in two kingdoms—one in this world with our physical being, and God's Kingdom with our spirit.

The kingdom of this world is fascinating, tempting, and enticing; however, it's fruit is always fleeting and shallow. Only lasting for so long. Jesus offered himself to us so that we could have all that is everlasting. Jesus at the cross is the pathway to freedom. Daily surrendering to God is my joy of the experience. I don't always get this right… but I fight for this surrender. Because I know—in it—I have the greatest of peace, that only He can provide.

> **Surrendering to God is aligning ourselves to seek the eternal and not the temporal of this broken world.**

To let go and let God is an ongoing, daily process of trusting God with our lives and choices and keeping our focus on the eternal.

This is not easy! Well… for me. It's not. The daily process. The daily dance of remembering where I need to surrender. It's like

THE ART OF SURRENDER, VULNERABILITY, & TRUST

trying to remind yourself 'hey there's someone else that can do this work for you—so why are you doing it!?'

So, how do we surrender to God? WHAT does that even look like?

Surrendering to God can be done by:

Your heart simply looking for God. Seeking Him.

Coming to Him in prayer and spending time in worship, His Word, or laying in His presence. Sitting in the stillness, and letting your hair down. Giving it all up, and giving it all to the One that can carry it for you. I have gotten more accomplished in shedding tears, and baring my soul on the carpet of my living room than probably anywhere else on earth.

Trusting God. Leaning not on our own understanding but trusting that God's ways (and timing) are truly better.

Understanding our amazing Identity in Christ. Knowing and accepting what it means to be a daughter or son of the King and embracing your true identity. In your worst lowest moments and days, you are royal! You are still loved, you are still His. Nothing can change this. Nothing can affect this. You belong to a God that designed every part of your entire being, and knows all the days of your life. He cares deeply for you, and the details of our lives that are important to us are important to Him.

Letting go and trusting God is making a choice—here's the choice thing again: moment by moment, giving it up to one who has it all figured out. Giving your life to God each day changes everything.

I know now that I could've surrendered so much that I held on to so tightly… I walked myself into so much pain trying to do it on my own. Even my thoughts, thinking and laboring over a thing for so long—when I could've let it go. Just in the letting go of my thinking—I could've had so much less to carry.

THE ART OF SURRENDER, VULNERABILITY, & TRUST

THE ART OF

PROPHECY WORDS & DRY BONES

THE ART OF PROPHECY, WORDS, & DRY BONES

Words. So easy to speak. Yet—a challenge to be aware of the responsibility that comes with them. Being careful and diligent with the words we use is such wisdom. **Words have creative power**, God demonstrated this for us to understand when He created the heavens and the earth with His words literally by speaking them into existence. What!? How mind blowing. Yes. Words are like God's paintbrushes. And to top that thought—We were created in the VERY image of God. Which means we have the authority of creating with our words as well. We can speak change, healing, and life into any situation. We can also speak death. Hi! I'm guilty. Guilty of rehearsing, repeating, and just non-productively using my words. The temptation is always there. We live in a world where words are used every day in the news, on social platforms, in music, and marketing to convey messages to us. We are always eating up words. And putting words back out into the atmosphere.

So what are we absorbing and what are we creating with all of these words? It's Something to consider. Your life may depend on it.

The Bible says life and death are in the power of the tongue.

Proverbs 18:21 puts it this way: "The tongue has the power of life and death." The stakes are high. Your words can either speak life, or your words can speak death. Our tongues can build others up, or they can tear them down.

I'm so thankful for the grace and willingness to want and to have a real revelation about words and their power. When I was at my very lowest desperate places—and had nothing much to use to change what was happening. I began to speak words over my life, over my children, over my finances, over just about anything. Again this was by faith, I chose to believe that my words could change my life. I can't stress enough—that any of the things that have saved my life were **CHOICES** I made in **FAITH**. Faith is not seeing with your natural eyes, but by a spirit of faith, just believing!

I stand here today to tell you, when I started to practice this consistently. Mountains moved. Things happened. And miracles became a normal part of my life. If you've never had a miracle happen—this is the breeding ground for you to start cultivating those miracles. When I started to see things happen—I began expecting more, and more! I began speaking more! And I saw my world change before my very eyes. Think of anything you started using and had great results, you're hooked. I am hooked on the power of words.

Here's a list of some of the words (Declarations) **I speak out loud** and I'll never stop. I have my children say them too. It may feel awkward at first—or sound strange for example to say 'I am healed' if you're battling an illness. But that is the point. By declaring you're healed, you're creating an atmosphere of healing! You're speaking and creating healing with your words. So get your word paintbrush and paint healing words all over yourself!

> *I am healed*
>
> *My body and mind lack nothing needed to work perfectly*
>
> *I will accomplish all of my goals*
>
> *I am the righteousness of Christ*
>
> *God is for me*
>
> *I am protected from sickness and disease*
>
> *I am whole*

I see truth

I am brave

I am victorious

I have all that I need to create a beautiful life

I will have healthy relationships

My soul is healed

I will live in abundance

My children will flourish in every area of their life

My children will have excellent health

Everything I touch will produce good things

I am filled with joy

I am filled with peace

I will always have enough

I will never lack anything

The best days of my life are ahead of me

I am filled with hope

I am an overcomer

The list goes on, but this is a start. Make it your own, it changes as life changes.

I prosper in all things. I remain in health, just as my soul prospers. (3 John 1:3)

Speak what you believe until you see what you say

I had a dream one night in 2016 that changed my life, and in it—God took me to a place that looked like a large endless valley of skeletons. He kept showing me all of these surrounding terrains filled with them, just a bunch of dry bones, and nothing was living. There were no trees, no water, no signs of life. I was so unsure of what this was while I was seeing this. I felt like I was supposed to help in some way, my heart was heavy, I didn't know what to do. I asked God what do you want me to do? Why are you showing me this? He said

Ezekiel 37. That's all I heard. I woke from my dream, it was about 3 am. I didn't know what Ezekiel 37 was, other than a chapter in the Bible. So I frantically got out my Bible and looked it up. At this time, during this year, I was struggling to find hope for my situation. As a single Mom, fighting to make things work, fighting depression, working multiple jobs, one child a toddler—the other with special needs. Life felt too heavy. I wanted to give up. I felt like I failed at the vision for my life. I was surrounded in circumstances that seemingly had no answers, just long term effects.

So when I opened my Bible. This is what I saw.

> *Ezekiel 37:1–10*
>
> ***The Lord took hold of me, and I was carried away by the Spirit of the Lord to a valley filled with bones. 2 He led me all around among the bones that covered the valley floor. They were scattered everywhere across the ground and were completely dried out. 3 Then he asked me, "Son of man, can these bones become living people again?"***

THE ART OF PROPHECY, WORDS, & DRY BONES

"O Sovereign Lord," I replied, "you alone know the answer to that."

4 Then he said to me, "Speak a prophetic message to these bones and say, 'Dry bones, listen to the word of the Lord! 5 This is what the Sovereign Lord says: Look! I am going to put breath into you and make you live again! 6 I will put flesh and muscles on you and cover you with skin. I will put breath into you, and you will come to life. Then you will know that I am the Lord.'"

7 So I spoke this message, just as he told me. Suddenly as I spoke, there was a rattling noise all across the valley. The bones of each body came together and attached themselves as complete skeletons. 8 Then as I watched, muscles and flesh formed over the bones. Then skin formed to cover their bodies, but they still had no breath in them.

9 Then he said to me, "Speak a prophetic message to

the winds, son of man. Speak a prophetic message and say, 'This is what the Sovereign Lord says: Come, O breath, from the four winds! Breathe into these dead bodies so they may live again.'"

10 So I spoke the message as he commanded me, and **breath came into their bodies.** *They all came to life and stood up on their feet—a great army.*

11 Then he said to me, "Son of man, these bones represent the people of Israel. They are saying, 'We have become old, dry bones—all hope is gone. Our nation is finished.' 12 **Therefore, prophesy** *to them and say, 'This is what the Sovereign Lord says: O my people, I will open your graves of exile and cause you to rise again. Then I will bring you back to the land of Israel. 13 When this happens, O my people, you will know that I am the Lord. 14 I will put my Spirit in you, and you will live again and return home to your own land. Then you will know that I, the Lord, have spoken, and I have done what I said. Yes, the Lord has spoken!'"*

Wow. So much to take in. First I realized—this was yet another miracle. I was overwhelmed with the reality that God took His time to give me this powerful encounter. The miracle of God hearing me, the miracle of being seen by Him. An ancient, answered prayer, to ask Him for help, and to never leave me. It was so comforting to know—that my life mattered enough—that He gave me a dream that quite frankly might have saved my life. I realized through this experience that I had to prophesy to myself, to my body, soul, and mind. I had to command myself to live. I took this and I ran with it. And I never looked back. I never will. I hope today you will too, *speak life* and command every area of your life that may seem dead, or hopeless to come alive! And watch God work through the power of the Holy Spirit. I'm speaking to anyone with depression, thoughts of suicide, or fear. You are not alone, and you have the power inside of you to overcome. Please get help if you are suffering, don't wait another hour, another day to get what you need to survive and let go of any shame that is holding you back from your breakthrough!

Psalm 33:6

"The LORD merely spoke, and the heavens were created. He breathed the word, and all the stars were born."

I again say, it's by total faith, that **I choose** to believe that what I say, and what I speak—will without any question—be. Faith has become so simple as I've walked through different seasons. Simple because of the revelation that Faith is a choice. A choice that saved my life.

Even if you have no faith right now, you can choose to take a leap into the unknown—and start speaking life over yourself—speak good things to yourself, speak hope and healing. And watch the power of words come to life. Speaking God's word and what He says about you will impact your faith, and make it grow. You have this miracle in your voice!

THE ART OF PROPHECY, WORDS, & DRY BONES

HEROES & INSPIRATION

THE ART OF HEROES & INSPIRATION

When you grow up in a somewhat non traditional way—You may not have role models to look up to. If your parents were divorced, if you happen to be adopted, maybe moved around a lot—never developing roots, or just in general never had the privilege of a solid, thriving environment filled with positive examples—having heroes, and role models to look up to have been important to me.

Anyone that knows me even a little, knows I love Oprah. When I was 16 years old, a request on my Christmas list was the Oprah's anniversary DVD Collection. Yes I'm an old soul, deep down. Always have been. Now I embrace this—when I was younger I didn't know why my friends weren't into some of the same things I was so passionate about. Now I get it. How do you write about why Oprah inspires you? I know the thing that struck me, and most all of our connections to a hero is, ***they did something you dream of doing, did something incredible for people... Or they overcame an obstacle, and you admire them deeply for it.***

Oprah.

A Philanthropist and entrepreneur, Oprah Winfrey has influenced culture on a global scale. Her long-running talk show, "The Oprah Winfrey Show," won dozens of Daytime Emmy Awards and featured interviews with over 35,000 people.

Winfrey's extensive history of philanthropy has given her a reputation as one of the most generous individuals in the world. In 2004, she became the first African-American woman to join Business Week's "Top Philanthropists" list. In a since-archived interview, she told Business Week, "I believe that to whom much is given, much is expected. So, I will continue to use my voice and my life as a catalyst for change, inspiring and encouraging people to help make a difference in the lives of others."

That part, using your *voice*.

At the 2018 Golden Globe Awards, Winfrey was honored with the Cecil B. DeMille Award, which recognizes "outstanding contributions to the world of entertainment." She became the first black woman to receive the award in its 66-year history.

In her acceptance speech, she recognized her impact saying, "There are some little girls watching as I become the first black woman to be given the same award. It is an honor and it is a privilege to share the evening with all of them."

She's the first in so many categories.

Besides being the first African-American woman to own her own production company, being television's highest-paid entertainer, being a producer of and actress in her own television shows, and being the host of one of history's most popular talk shows (reaching over 15 million people daily), she's also a powerful advocate for women, and people in need.

Here's a really short honorary list of women particularly that offered inspiration to me in various ways. The list goes on and continues to grow.

Amy Schafer—My Pastor, Grace Life Church Pittsburgh

Princess Diana

Dame Zaha Hadid

Cleopatra

Christine Caine

Harriet Tubman

Hedy Lamarr

Sally Ride

Augusta Savage

Georgia O'Keefe

Annie Leibovitz

Ava Duvernay

THE ART OF HEROES & INSPIRATION

Florence Nightingale

Queen Rania Al-Abdullah

Queen Esther

Mary, Mother of Jesus

Anne Frank

If you look up any of these women up you'll find courage, overcoming, power, raw talent, lots of hard work and even bravery.

Who inspires you, and why?

_____

_____

_____

_____

_____

_____

Take a moment to reflect on inspiring people, study the intimate details, and history of their journey.

I believe humans are hardwired for heroism & inspiration. The heroic is an imprint that's been deposited inside all of us because we're made in the image of God. Even though that imprint has been distorted by the fall of man, it is something that remains. We know what's good, right, and true. We know the exhilaration and blessing that comes naturally when we help, serve, and do anything to uplift one another. There's nothing like the warmth and reward of overcoming an obstacle to serve, enhance, or better someone's life. This is the **God DNA** inside every one of us. To pave the way, to rise above or overcome while facing adversity is powerful.

God is jealous for our love, attention and destiny. Most of our collective destinations include loving ourselves well so we can love and serve others, and being the answer someone else needs.

Learning how to serve humanity with the giftings God gave us, is heroic work.

A prayer that changes everything.

A PRAYER THAT CHANGES EVERYTHING

Dear God,

I've been through a lot of things I don't understand. I don't have all the answers. I don't know how to express my brokenness, my disappointments, I feel the pains of life.

I need your help, I need your power. I need your love.

I want to know you, like you know me. I accept this love, I accept that you sent your only son, Jesus, here to this earth to make a way for me to know you, and live this life with you not just now but forever—even when this life is over.

I accept you, I need saved, save me. I need freedom. I need a fresh start. A new beginning. Be with me, heal me, show me who you are.

Let me feel and know your love. Let me see myself through your eyes, change me from the inside out. Take all of my pain, my shame, my questions and all that I don't understand in this life—I leave it all with you at your feet… I trust you with it all.

I pray this prayer by my own choice—by faith—God I choose life, I choose you, and choose to believe that I can have life with unconditional love through the gift of your son Jesus, my savior.

In Jesus name I pray this life changing—never to be the same again—prayer. I give it all up today. Take my heart into your hands, and never let me go. Amen.

This is the prayer that changes everything.

Your life is forever now safely in God's hands.

If you prayed this prayer for the first time, please write to me—and let me know how I can continue to pray for you and celebrate you in this new journey! Write down today's date. It's one of the best days of your life.

A PRAYER THAT CHANGES EVERYTHING

THE ART OF

Writing It All Down

There is such importance in

Writing Things Down

And then God answered: "Write this. Write what you see. Write it out in big block letters so that it can be read on the run. This vision-message is a witness pointing to what's coming. It aches for the coming—it can hardly wait! And it doesn't lie. If it seems slow in coming, wait. It's on its way. It will come right on time." (Habakkuk 2:2)

Writing things down helps the information stick. Like, really stick. It brings my (your) thoughts to life in a different way. It creates anticipation. Writing for me has become a never ending vision board for life.

Where would we be without writing? The writings of others have served as pillars of all cultures and influence to society. From history to novels, music, politics, religion and film. Writing begins a process and influences across all of human history.

Writing things down takes our listening, thinking and reading a step further. The simple act of writing forces us to think about what it is that we are going through, hearing or feeling.

When we take any notes it helps us to recall the information later right? Like studying for an exam or preparing a presentation for work. Even a shopping list can be a game changer instead of winging it by memory.

How many times have you written a list only to find out that you didn't even have to refer to it? But try not writing that same list, and chances are that you will forget many of the items. I am the queen of sticky note trails… and buying fun looking journals for every quarter of the year. The process of writing anything down has helped me to remember. Even if it's a random inspiration. It matters.

And that is the part, remembering. We need to write things down *to remember*—even for those of us with a good memory.

Exodus 17:14 (NLT) says, "…the Lord instructed Moses, "Write this down on a scroll as a permanent reminder…"

Jeremiah 30:2 (AMP) says, "This says the Lord, the God of Israel: Write all the words that I have spoken to you in a book."

Psalm 105:5 tells us to "remember" *the wonders* God has done...

Psalm 103:2 tells us to bless the Lord and "forget not" all his benefits.

So by not forgetting we bless God!

If God says to "remember" and "forget not", then we can safely assume we naturally do. Life is busy, things get lost in translation! Years fly past us. Let's face it—we live in a super speed paced world. Write not only for the sake of remembering important things, but for our hearts to transcribe emotions, and a help the decluttering of the soul.

I've also heard it said that writing things down can also give the Holy Spirit something to work with. In John 14:26 it says that the Holy Spirit will "remind" us. Writing will act as a reference to which the Holy Spirit may even trigger us to go back and look at. I have been reminded on SEVERAL occasions of notes I had taken on a message or even during my quiet times, and I've been thankful that I have had my journals and notebooks that I can refer back to revisit what it was that I needed to see again. Sometimes God will give us something now that we are going to need to use later. He may be preparing us in advance for things that we are yet to face. Those thoughts are often a reminder from the Holy Spirit.

Writing things down can be a resource for others…

Besides serving as a reference for us to use later, our notes may even be a beneficial resource for others at some point in the future, had it not been for many being inspired by God to write down accounts, we would not have the Bible. We never know what our notes may lead us or others to in the future! This little book of mine actually wouldn't exist without my journals filled with notes. There is no way I could've remembered some things without having written it down.

It's kind of fun to go back through and look at different seasons of life and see how far you've come. It's also amazing to see examples of God talking to me even though I didn't know that's what that was at the time. Journals can show evidence of our growth, that we might otherwise overlook.

We can see how David did this too in the Bible. David was the primary author of the majority of the Psalms. The Psalms contain a combination of cries to God in times of despair, praise to God in times of celebration and confessions to God of sin along with pleadings for forgiveness. There are a vast range of emotions recorded throughout the book of Psalms. After having written down the events and the corresponding emotions and prayers that went with them, I'm positive David was able to look back over them and see how far he'd come and how much he had grown. I especially loved to read and meditate on the Psalms when I was going through very difficult times in my life. It was so encouraging, and touched my heart deeply to know the depths of another's journey—and seeing them transparently cry out to God. Others, throughout history all the way to present times, have been able to benefit from his notes and writings and by seeing his growth from boy to man, from despair to joy, and from sin to forgiveness and victory. We can follow David's example of writing things down in order to see our own transformations.

Write prayers.

Write about dreams.

Write out pain.

Write breakthroughs.

Write the future.

Write your history.

Write all you can.

It doesn't have to be published in a book, but it can be your own tool of reflection and serve as an incredible gift to your life.

So now it's your turn.

I hope I inspired you to write just a little or maybe a LOT, and see the beauty wrapped up in the gift of putting things into words.

THE ART OF

Writing It All Down

THE ART OF BEING BROKEN

THE ART OF WRITING IT ALL DOWN

THE ART OF BEING BROKEN

THE ART OF WRITING IT ALL DOWN

THE ART OF WRITING IT ALL DOWN

THE ART OF WRITING IT ALL DOWN

THE ART OF WRITING IT ALL DOWN

THE ART OF BEING BROKEN

THE ART OF WRITING IT ALL DOWN

THE ART OF BEING BROKEN

THE ART OF WRITING IT ALL DOWN

THE ART OF WRITING IT ALL DOWN

THE ART OF WRITING IT ALL DOWN

THE ART OF BEING BROKEN

THE ART OF WRITING IT ALL DOWN

THE ART OF WRITING IT ALL DOWN

THE ART OF BEING BROKEN

THE ART OF WRITING IT ALL DOWN

THE ART OF WRITING IT ALL DOWN

THE ART OF WRITING IT ALL DOWN

THE ART OF WRITING IT ALL DOWN

THE ART OF BEING BROKEN

THE ART OF WRITING IT ALL DOWN

THE ART OF BEING BROKEN

THE ART OF WRITING IT ALL DOWN

THE ART OF BEING BROKEN

THE ART OF WRITING IT ALL DOWN

THE ART OF WRITING IT ALL DOWN

THE ART OF WRITING IT ALL DOWN

THE ART OF WRITING IT ALL DOWN

THE ART OF WRITING IT ALL DOWN

THE ART OF WRITING IT ALL DOWN

THE ART OF WRITING IT ALL DOWN

THE ART OF WRITING IT ALL DOWN

www.ingramcontent.com/pod-product-compliance
Lightning Source LLC
Chambersburg PA
CBHW081409080526
44589CB00016B/2512